The Best of Japanese Culture

Stuart Varnam-Atkin

IBC Publishing

Introduction

Why 108?
What is *igo*?
What are *ema*?
What are *kokeshi*?
What does 7-5-3 mean?
Why are carp streamers flown?
Do shrine priests really play football?
Why are noodles eaten on December 31st?
How many beads are there on a Buddhist rosary?

Since the lifting of the severe travel restrictions imposed during the Covid pandemic and the delayed 2020 Olympic Games in Tokyo, more and more visitors from all over the world have been flocking to Japan to experience its rich culture in person.

And it is a culture that offers something fascinating for people of any age and nationality. Many people can't wait to see the awesome Mt. Fuji and the famous historical buildings of Kyoto and Nara, the ancient capital cities. Others are most interested in Japanese cuisine and traditional customs. There is also, of course, a great interest these days in modern cultural features, such as 'maid cafes', *manga* and *anime*. But one thing all visitors tend to feel is the wonderful way in which many elements of traditional Japan and a whole host of seasonal attractions continue to co-exist with the ultra-modern.

This little book tries to answer some of the mountain of questions that foreigners ask by presenting a broad selection of colorful aspects of Japanese culture that can still be seen and experienced all over the country today. It includes short explanations of each item and carefully selected photographs that will give a vivid visual idea of Japanese life to those who have never experienced it, as well as providing fond memories for those who have been lucky enough to visit Japan.

The first five chapters present broad themes such as Shrines & Temples, Ceremonial Occasions and Features of Traditional Life. Chapter 6 presents images of seasonal events occurring throughout the year from early Spring through to the New Year. Japanese terms are distinguished by italics the first time they appear in each item. I hope you will find the text interesting and the photos a pleasure to look at.

For valuable insights, I am greatly indebted to Sumie Page and the priests and staff of Kotohira Shrine in Shikoku, as well as the staff and performers of the National Bunraku Theatre in Osaka and Tokyo. My sincere thanks go to Yoko Toyozaki for her careful research, and to Kyoko Kagawa and Hiromi Hishiki at IBC for their enthusiasm and support.

Stuart Varnam-Atkin
Kanagawa, Japan,
Marine Day, July 2024

Contents

Introduction.....2

Chapter 1   Shrines & Temples

Jinja 神社.....6

Shimenawa しめ縄.....7

Torii 鳥居.....8

Komainu 狛犬.....10

Saisenbako 賽銭箱.....11

Kemari 蹴鞠.....12

Tera 寺.....12

Goju-no-to 五重塔.....13

Kane 鐘.....15

Ema 絵馬.....16

O-mikuji おみくじ.....17

O-mamori お守り.....18

O-jizo-sama お地蔵さま.....19

Chapter 2   Out & About

Koban 交番.....21

Maneki-neko 招き猫.....21

Noren のれん.....22

Nawa-noren 縄のれん.....23

Chochin 提灯.....23

Shokuhin sanpuru 食品サンプル.....24

Daruma だるま.....25

Kokeshi こけし.....26

Maiko 舞妓.....27

Chapter 3   Ceremonial Occasions & Items

Shinzen-kekkonshiki 神前結婚式.....28

Tsuno-kakushi 角隠し.....31

Shio 塩.....31

Juzu 数珠.....32

Mokugyo 木魚.....33

Mizuhiki 水引.....34

Noshi のし.....35

Chapter 4   Games

Shogi 将棋.....36

Go 碁.....37

Hanetsuki 羽根つき.....38

Koma こま.....38

Tako たこ.....40

Sugoroku すごろく.....40

Karuta かるた.....41

Uta-garuta 歌がるた.....42

Hanafuda 花札.....43

Chapter 5　Features of Traditional Life

Ukiyo-e 浮世絵.....*44*

Noh 能.....*46*

Kyogen 狂言.....*46*

Bunraku 文楽.....*47*

Men 面.....*47*

Niwa 庭.....*48*

Bonsai 盆栽.....*49*

Kakejiku 掛け軸.....*50*

Ikebana 生け花.....*50*

Shiro 城.....*52*

Tenshukaku 天守閣.....*53*

Chapter 6　Seasonal Features

Momo-no-sekku 桃の節句.....*54*

Hina-ningyo ひな人形.....*54*

Hanami 花見.....*56*

Koinobori こいのぼり.....*57*

Gogatsu-ningyo 五月人形.....*58*

Tanabata-kazari 七夕飾り.....*59*

Hanabi 花火.....*60*

Mikoshi 神輿.....*61*

Bon-kazari 盆飾り.....*62*

Sensu 扇子.....*62*

Uchiwa うちわ.....*63*

Sudare & Yoshizu すだれ／よしず.....*64*

Kakigori かき氷.....*64*

Kaya 蚊帳.....*65*

Katori-senko 蚊取り線香.....*65*

Furin 風鈴.....*66*

Momiji-gari 紅葉狩り.....*67*

Tsukimi 月見.....*68*

Shichi-go-san 七五三.....*69*

Chitose-ame 千歳飴.....*70*

Botamochi & Ohagi ぼたもち（おはぎ）.....*70*

Kadomatsu 門松.....*71*

Shime-kazari しめ飾り.....*72*

Mochitsuki もちつき.....*72*

Kagami-mochi 鏡もち.....*73*

Toshikoshi-soba 年越しそば.....*74*

Joya-no-kane 除夜の鐘.....*74*

Hatsu-mode 初詣.....*75*

Hamaya 破魔矢.....*76*

O-toso おとそ.....*76*

O-toshidama お年玉.....*78*

O-sechi-ryori おせち料理.....*78*

Kamakura かまくら.....*79*

Jinja
神社

Normal Shinto shrines connected with ancestor worship are called *jinja*, often including the suffix *–miya* in the name. However, several other names are used, depending on the status and history of the shrine. *Taisha* is a very sacred name, as in Izumo Taisha in Shimane Prefecture. High-ranked shrines closely connected with an emperor or enshrining a past emperor are called *jingu*, as in Meiji Jingu in Tokyo and Ise Jingu in Mie Prefecture. The suffix *–gu* also suggests Imperial family connections, as in Tsurugaoka Hachimangu in Kamakura.

Shimenawa
しめ縄

At the entrance and elsewhere in the shrine grounds, you will see *shimenawa* twisted straw ropes from which hang strips of white paper (*shide*). They indicate the edge of a sacred place and are sometimes hung around sacred trees and rocks.

The approach to a shrine is indicated by at least one *torii* symbolic gateway. Like the roofed lychgate of an old English church, the first torii marks the border between the everyday and sacred worlds. The number of torii is not fixed. You should pass through them to cleanse your heart and mind ready to appear before the enshrined god or gods. Always keep to the side of the path leading to the shrine as the center is reserved for the deities.

Torii
鳥居

Torii have been described as one of the finest artistic creations formed by just four intersecting lines. The characters for 'torii' literally mean 'bird-perch.' Neither the origin of the name or the design is clear. Like the English word 'door', the name may be derived from the old Indian word *torana*, meaning 'gate.' Torii closely resemble gateways found in China and Korea, but they may simply have developed from ancient gateways similar to the *mon* gateways still found in front of old houses and temple precincts.

Torii are constructed of *hinoki* (cypress) wood, stone, metal or concrete. There are more than a dozen main design variations, most of them with two posts (*hashira*), a top lintel (*kasagi*) and a tie-beam (*nuki*) connecting the posts. They range from the colossal,

stark modern steel 1st Torii at Yasukuni Jinja in Tokyo, with its straight *shimmei*-style kasagi and nuki, to the famous and more elaborate red *ryobu*-style torii at Itsukushima Shrine at Miyajima, near Hiroshima, which stands in the sea. Fushimi Inari Shrine in Kyoto has tunnels formed by thousands of red torii. In the case of Tsurugaoka Hachimangu in Kamakura, the three torii are a great distance apart because many worshippers used to arrive at Kamakura by ship and walked up to the shrine from the beach.

Komainu
狛犬

At each side of the entrance to a shrine there are often two stone, wooden or bronze statues of mythical guardian beasts resembling lions. Called *komainu*, they ward off evil. In the case of Inari shrines dedicated to the god of the harvest and industry, the statues are of foxes. The pathways to the shrine are lined by *toro* stone lanterns, usually donated by devotees. Near the shrine buildings there is a roofed water trough (*chozuya* or *temizuya*) where you wash your hands and rinse out your mouth using one of the ladles (*hishaku*) provided. Note that you should not drink from the ladle but pour water into your cupped hand.

Saisenbako
賽銭箱

Shrine buildings tend to be simple in appearance, often undecorated. They are designed for worshipping the gods, not for preaching by priests. The main buildings are the *Haiden* Outer Hall or Oratory for public worship and the *Honden* Inner Sanctuary, which contains symbolic objects of worship and is out of bounds to the general public. In front of the Haiden there is always a money box for offerings (*saisenbako*) and a rope with small bells hanging from the roof. You throw in some money (usually coins), pull the rope, clap twice to attract the attention of the gods and then pray with your hands lifted to face level.

Kemari
蹴鞠

The ancient amusement called *kemari* shows the long history of Asian soccer skills! Probably introduced from China in the 7th century, it can still be seen at several shrines, such as Shimogamo Jinja in Kyoto, where it's played by the priests to pray for peace and a good harvest to kick off the New Year. The 2014 event featured an official World Cup match ball. The circle of usually eight players (*mariashi*) wearing colorful ancient court costumes and leather shoes shout "Ari", "Ya" and "Oh" as they kick a deerskin ball (*mari*) to each other, keeping it in the air as long as possible. Any part of the body can be used apart from the hands and arms. The aim is to please the deities said to be watching from the pine, cherry, willow and maple trees around the 'pitch'.

Kemari can also be seen at Kotohira Shrine (Kompira-san) in Shikoku in May, July and December. Not to be missed!

Tera
寺

Tera is the general term for a Buddhist temple. Temple names generally end in *-ji* (Sensoji in Tokyo, Todaiji in Nara) or *-in* (Chion-in in Kyoto). Up to the 19th century, shrines and temples were often combined, and architectural features of both can sometimes be found in the same location, such as the five-story pagoda in Itsukushima Shrine on the island of Miyajima. However, temples are distinguished by more flamboyant designs than Shinto shrines, and many sacred objects such as statues, bell towers, and pagodas.

Goju-no-to
五重塔

The design and names of temple buildings vary according to the sect. Most large temples have an impressive *Sanmon* main gate, a *Kondo* (also called *Hondo* or *Butsuden*) Main Hall, in which statues are kept, and a *Kodo* (or *Hatto*) Lecture Hall, where Buddhist scriptures are read. The other distinctive temple structure is the

pagoda, often with five stories (*goju-no-to*). Like the India *stupa* from which their design evolved, pagodas hold holy relics. Recent research has proved that goju-no-to, supported by a central pillar, are remarkably earthquake-resistant. They cannot be entered like church or cathedral towers.

Kane
鐘

A hanging bell is called a *tsuri-gane* and temple bells are known as *bonsho*. However, technically speaking, bonsho are not 'bells' at all, but gongs; they are not rung by a swinging clapper but by a direct hit from the outside by a suspended wooden beam (*shumoku*). This is sometimes so large that it needs several people to swing it. Bonsho are housed in a special roofed belfry called a *shoro* (or *kane-tsuki-do*), separate from the main temple buildings.

In the past, major temple bells were rung 108 times every morning and evening. Sometimes they also marked the time; the bell at Zojoji Temple in Edo (Tokyo) was rung every afternoon to call the mendicant monks back to the temple. In the quieter days of the past, it was said some bells could be heard dozens of kilometers away. Edo had more than 300 large temple bells at one time.

Ema
絵馬

Ema are small votive wooden tablets on sale at shrines. They are usually around 15 cms wide and five-sided like a cross-section of a house, often with a little roof at the top and cords attached for hanging. You write a wish on one and leave it at the shrine. Ema were originally offered as gratitude to the gods, but today they are more often used for making wishes. Thousands of ema bearing wishes for examination success can be seen at shrines dedicated to education. There are also large ema available for group wishes.

O-mikuji
おみくじ

O-mikuji (divine fortune) are written fortunes available at both shrines and temples for a small fee. The normal process is to pull or shake a bamboo stick out of a cylinder or a box. It's marked with a number and a priest or shrine maiden (*miko*) will hand you the corresponding paper that explains your fortune. However, there are now many o-mikuji vending machines that look rather like red mail boxes.

O-mamori
お守り

The word *mamori* means 'defence or protection,' and an *o-mamori* (or *mayoke*) is a kind of small talisman or amulet from a shrine or a temple to bring good luck and ward off evil. It consists of a piece of paper, wood or cloth blessed by a priest. It bears the name of the god and a prayer and is enclosed in a small brocade bag bearing the name of the shrine or temple. O-mamori generally have a specific application: to provide safety from traffic accidents; protection from illness; safe childbirth; success in examinations; etc. They can be carried around or hung somewhere, such as on a car dashboard. They are sometimes given as presents when someone returns from a visit to a famous shrine or temple.

O-jizo-sama
お地蔵さま

The stone *o-jizo-sama* statues seen beside roads all over Japan portray Jizo Bosatsu, the Buddhist savior believed to relieve people from all kinds of suffering. He is the guardian deity of travelers and pregnant women, and protects deceased children from demons. He appears as a monk with a shaved head wearing pilgrim's sandals, and there is the faintest of smiles on his face. In his left hand is a mystic jewel that grants wishes (*hoju*), and in his right hand a staff (*shakujo*) with six metal rings; pilgrims would jingle these as they walked along so that living creatures could hear them coming and get out of the way unharmed.

Local people often hang some item of clothing, such as a bib, around the statue's neck or shoulders and put a knitted hat or hood on his head.

Koban
交番

Koban is the common name for the small police boxes that serve as local branch offices of large district police stations. They are manned by between one and a dozen or more policemen (*omawari-san*) on a shift basis. They are generally small two-story structures, some with a striking modern design. There is an office at the front with local maps on the wall and sleeping accommodation above. The versions built on the front of the local policeman's house, mostly in rural areas, are known as *chuzaisho* rather than koban.

Maneki-neko
招き猫

Ornamental *maneki-neko* (beckoning cats) have been popular since the middle of the Edo period as good-luck talismans. Made of clay, porcelain, papier-mâche, wood, or plastic, they are believed to bring good business to shops and restaurants. They are also often displayed as a sign of welcome in the *genkan* entrance of houses. The cats beckon in Japanese-style, with the palm facing outward. Those with the right paw raised are believed to bring good luck in business finance; those with the left paw raised are for welcoming customers or guests. The cats are usually holding an oval gold coin (called a *koban*) from the Edo period.

Noren
のれん

Noren are split curtains made of cloth still hung at the entrance to traditional-style restaurants, shops and public baths. They started off as lengths of cloth that provided shade and kept the street dust from entering the door, like the curtains used in temples. The name of the establishment (*yago*) and maybe the family crest (*mon*) is usually printed on the noren, so in the old days they were the equivalent of the *kanban* signs now seen on the sides of commercial buildings. When the noren is hanging outside, it's a sign that the place is open for business. Noren bearing actors' names traditionally hang at the entrance to theater dressing-rooms.

Nawa-noren
縄のれん

There are several words for casual drinking and eating establishments, including *izakaya* (remain + liquor store; i.e. drinking at a liquor store), *akachochin* (red lanterns), and *nomiya* (drinking place). Another term,

less heard these days, is *nawa-noren*, after a special type of noren made of many straw cords hanging over the entrance. The phrase *nawa-noren o kuguru* (go under the straw cords) used to be a common phrase for going for some cheap drink and food.

Chochin
提灯

Chochin are paper lanterns for outside use that can be hung from the eaves or carried. They can still be seen in many colors and sizes all over Japan and serve many different purposes, although today they usually contain an electric light bulb rather than the traditional candle.

They are generally made of tough paper attached to collapsible bamboo hoops. Many chochin, especially red ones (*akachochin*), hang outside restaurants and

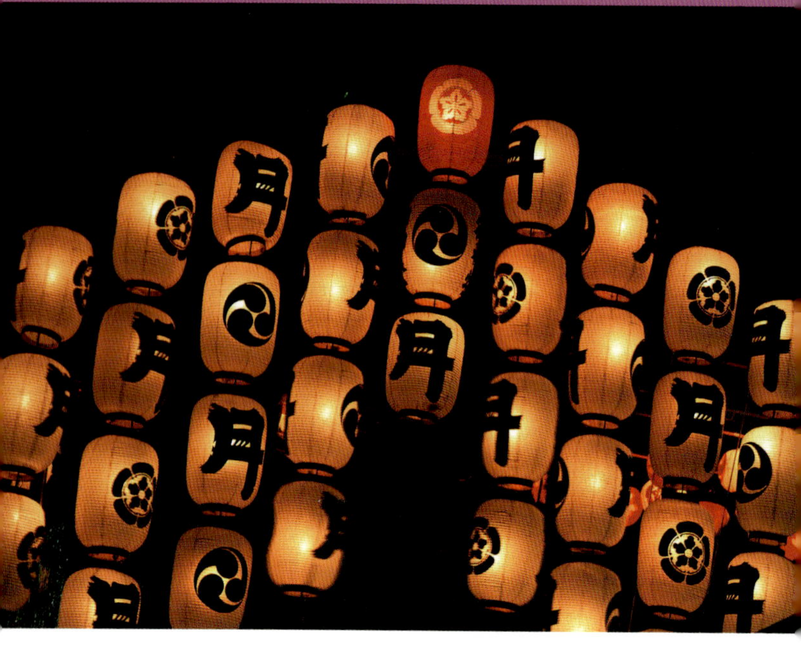

drinking places to advertise the establishment's name or what it serves. White and yellow chochin can often be seen at shrines and temples, and in festivals they may bear patrons' names.

Shokuhin sanpuru
食品サンプル

Many restaurants have display windows featuring realistic models of many of the dishes and drinks on the menu, plus their prices. This is especially true of the restaurant floor of department stores, where the idea originated. A fine display draws customers, and even if you can't read the menu, you can always go outside and point at a model!

The hand-painted models are called *shokuhin sanpuru* (food sample). This sensible idea was developed

in Tokyo in the early 20th century as unusual dishes from overseas began to appear. The models used to be made of wax, but today silicon molds of actual food items are taken and then liquid vinyl models are made.

Daruma
だるま

Legless, armless, neckless *daruma* dolls made of wood, plastic, stone or papier-mâche over a bamboo frame can be seen all over Japan. They often have a rounded, weighted base so that they will always roll back upright when tipped over, symbolizing a spirit of never giving up. The name comes from the Indian Buddhist priest Boddhidharma, regarded as the founder of Zen

Buddhism, who traveled to China in the 6th century. He is said to have meditated staring at a wall for nine years until he was unable to use his legs, and he cut off his eyelids so that he would never doze off. The common red color of daruma dolls is based on an Indian priest's dress.

Kokeshi
こけし

Kokeshi are a unique type of cylindrical wooden doll with a rounded head and no arms or legs. Kokeshi carving developed as a winter activity of woodcarvers and farmers in the Tohoku region of northern Japan in the 19th century. Traditional dolls have hand-painted faces and floral kimono designs, mostly red with black hair and simple facial features, though some are painted entirely in black. The head is often removable; some Miyagi Prefecture dolls let out a charming squeak when it's revolved. Kokeshi are made from various types of wood with a nice grain, *sakura* cherry wood being popular. They develop a pleasant patina with age and should occasionally be polished with a soft cotton *tenugui* towel. Kokeshi-shaped ornaments include toothpick-holders, pencils, erasers and mobile phone straps.

Maiko
舞妓

Maiko are young female entertainers, usually in their late teens, who entertain guests at private parties in Kyoto by performing traditional music, dancing and singing, pouring drinks, and playing games. They can easily be recognized by their distinctive appearance: colorful kimonos with seasonal motifs, very long drooping sashes, fancy ornamental hairpins (*kanzashi*), and high platform sandals like clogs. They also use traditional makeup: red and black on a white foundation like a mask. They are actually undergoing rigorous training to become a *geiko*, the name used in Kyoto for geisha. These days, many female visitors to Kyoto, Japanese and foreign, enjoy dressing up as a maiko for the day.

Shinzen-kekkonshiki
神前結婚式

Many Japanese hold a traditional Shinto *shinzen-kekkonshiki* wedding ceremony, attended by a *kannushi* priest, *miko* shrine maidens, and close family members and friends. The couple wear formal wedding kimonos (*kekkon-isho*). The groom (*hanamuko*) wears a kimono with gray split-trousers (*hakama*) and a long, loose

black jacket (*haori*) bearing his family crest (*mon*). For the official ceremony the bride (*hanayome*) wears a long overgarment (*uchikake*) over a white wedding kimono (*shiromuku*). White is traditionally the color of death in Japan, so it symbolizes both the death of the bride's natural ties to her parents and a willingness to dye the garment in the color of her husband's family. She may change into a colorful *iro-uchikake* kimono before the reception as a sign she has become a member of her husband's family, and change again during the party into a Western dress, just to be fashionable!

Tsuno-kakushi
角隠し

A bride's hair is arranged in a traditional *bunkin-takashimada* style with various ornamental hairpins. Instead of a Western-style veil, there are two choices of hair covering. One is a large white band called a *tsuno-kakushi* (horn-cover) which is said to hide a woman's 'horns' and indicate her obedience to her husband, although most brides these days probably never think of the symbolism! The tsuno-kakushi is often worn at the start of the reception party as well. The other covering is a kind of large white silk bonnet called a *wataboshi*, designed so that the bride's face is only properly visible to her husband. This is usually removed before the reception.

Shio
塩

Salt is regarded as the great element of purification in Japan; it is believed to be effective in providing balance, warding off evil spirits, and generating strength. It features in many Shinto rites. One example is the salt thrown by sumo wrestlers before each bout to purify both themselves and the ring (*dohyo*). Salt is also sprinkled on an empty plot of land at a ground-breaking ceremony (*jichinsai*) to pacify the god of the soil. Another example is *mori-jio*, small conical mounds of salt placed on a saucer at one or both sides of the entrance to a house to purify all those who enter. Similar piles are sometimes seen outside restaurants today.

Juzu

数珠

A *juzu* (counting beads) is a Buddhist rosary that believers hold in their hand for counting while repeating the *Namu-amidabutsu* chant, or wear round their neck. A complete rosary is a ring of 108 beads (*honren-juzu* or *nirin-juzu*), representing the 108 earthly desires which should be avoided. There are shorter versions with 54, 42, 27, 21, or 14 beads and larger ones with up to 1,080 beads. The beads are generally made from sandalwood, nuts, or quartz, and come in different sizes. The tassels on the juzu represent we humans who have those desires. The way the beads are strung together varies depending on the sect. Many people carry a small juzu when they visit a grave or attend a Buddhist funeral (*soshiki*) or memorial service (*hoji*). Kyoto is the main center of juzu production.

Mokugyo
木魚

A *mokugyo* (wooden fish) is a rounded wooden drum used during the chanting of Buddhist sutras, both in temples and at private homes. Struck rhythmically like a gong, it produces a mellow kind of sound. Carved from a single piece of wood, often camphorwood, mokugyo usually sit on a small *zabuton* cushion and are in the shape of a fat fish. With a slit at one end to represent the fish's mouth and often carved with fish scales, mokugyo

are related historically to the hanging wooden fish used as dinner gongs at Zen temples. There is a rounded handle at one end, which may be intricately carved; some handles have a design of dragons holding a sacred jewel. The end of the wooden beater is padded with cloth, rubber or leather. Some mokugyo resemble a human skull.

Mizuhiki
水引

Japan has a long tradition of wrapping presents carefully and beautifully. This denotes respect, and also reflects the practice of presents not being opened in the presence of the giver. Formal gifts are covered in a sheet of high quality white paper called *hoshogami* and then tied with *mizuhiki* cords and decorated with a *noshi*. Mizuhiki are stiff cords made from mulberry pulp paper which has been soaked in the water used to rinse rice and then hardened. Sometimes mizuhiki are made into complex designs of lucky creatures such as cranes and turtles to accompany the betrothal gifts exchanged by families before a wedding.

Noshi
のし

Noshi (short for *noshiawabi*, stretched abalone) is a lucky decoration added to the special envelope for gifts of money at weddings or funerals (*noshibukuro*) or the white paper wrapper that goes around a gift. Always placed in the upper right corner, it originally consisted of a folded red and white paper envelope holding a strip of dried abalone (*awabi*). These days a strip of yellow paper is generally used instead, or the noshi is printed on the wrapper or envelope (*noshigami*). There is often a message printed on the noshigami, such as *Go-kekkon iwai* (Congratulations on your marriage), but if you want a message-free noshigami wrapper you can ask for *muji-noshi*.

Shogi
将棋

The two major board games in Japan are *shogi* and *igo* (often called just *go*). They are both for two players and are extremely popular, particularly with men.

Shogi is very similar to chess, the aim being to checkmate the opponent's king (*osho*). Each player begins with 20 five-sided pointed pieces, all bearing a name written in kanji characters. There are equivalents of rooks, bishops, knights and pawns, but no queens. The two major differences from chess are the ability to use captured pieces and change the strength of pieces when they are inside enemy territory. The board has 81 squares (9×9).

Go

碁

The ancient game of *go* developed from the Chinese game of Wei-chi around the 6th century. Regarded by many as an art, it's played with disk-shaped black and white stones (*ishi*). There are 181 black 'crow' stones made from a kind of slate—for the player who starts the game—and 180 white 'heron' stones traditionally made from shell. They are kept in round wooden pots called *goke*, *goki* or *gotsubo*. The traditional wooden board (*goban*) is marked out with a mesh of black lacquered lines to create 361 (19×19) intersecting points (*me* or *moku*) on which the players place stones in turn. The aim is to gain territory and capture your opponents' stones by surrounding them. There are said to be more possible moves than all the atoms in the universe!

Hanetsuki
羽根つき

At one time, a common sound on the streets on New Year's Day was the 'kon-kon' of shuttlecocks (*hane*) being hit by wooden battledores (*hagoita*) in a game resembling badminton. However, no net is used; the idea is simply to keep the shuttlecock in the air. Mostly played by girls dressed in kimono, it's called *hanetsuki*. Today, however, you rarely hear the sound because most children are more interested in modern pursuits such as video games, and it's also become more dangerous to play out on the streets. Hagoita remain popular in the form of lucky ornaments for display (*kazari-hagoita*), especially at the New Year, with topical designs featuring famous sportspeople, politicians, actors, TV stars, and manga and anime characters.

Koma
こま

Tops (*koma*) have been spinning in Japan for well over 1,000 years. Wooden tops unearthed from 8th century ruins show that they had entered Japan from China and Korea by the Nara period. Made of wood, bamboo, metal or plastic, they come in many shapes and sizes; some have a protruding rod for spinning with the fingers, others use strings, and some even make pleasant humming sounds. Top-spinning became a feature of New Year festivities around the end of the 19th century.

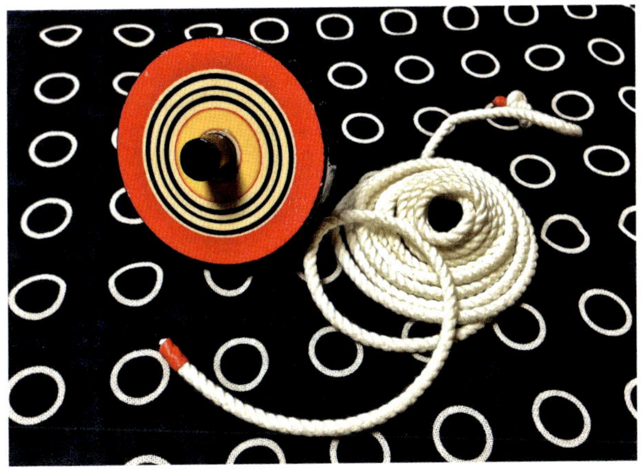

Tako
たこ

The Japanese word for a kite is *tako*. Kite-flying (*tako-age*) used to be a popular outdoor activity at the New Year, although it is not seen so much today. However, many people still enjoy flying kites  all year round, and major kite competitions are held in various locations. Kites have long been treasured for their artistic value, and they make stunning souvenirs.

Kites have a long history in Japan and they have been used in various ways. Originally they had the religious meaning of linking heaven and earth. Later, they were used by military commanders for sending messages, and by samurai to announce the birth of a baby boy. During the Edo period, many different designs and shapes evolved: dragons, lions, warriors, woodblock print images (*nishiki-e-dako*), figures, masks, calligraphy, birds and insects.

Sugoroku
すごろく

Sugoroku (double six) is a dice and board game that has gone through many changes over the centuries and has been compared to backgammon, pachisi, ludo, Monopoly and snakes-and-ladders! There are ancient board versions

(*ban-sugoroku*) as well as many types using a picture trail (*e-sugoroku*). In the Shoso-in Treasure House of Todaiji Temple in Nara, you can see a board used by the 45th emperor, Shomu, in the 8th century. It's a game that today is often given away with children's magazines, featuring topical personalities and cartoon characters.

Karuta
かるた

The term *karuta* (from the Portuguese word *carta*) refers to several types of cards featuring pictures, numbers or calligraphy that are used for playing various card games, especially at the New Year. Today there are many sets to help children learn Japanese and foreign languages, including English.

Playing cards (now called *toranpu*) were introduced to Japan by Portuguese sailors visiting Nagasaki in the 16th century. Long before that, however, Japanese nobles were playing games in which the two halves of clamshells had to be matched (*kai-awase*).

Uta-garuta
歌がるた

In the 13th century, the poet Fujiwara no Teika created a famous anthology of 100 great 31-syllable *waka* poems titled *Ogura Hyakunin-isshu* (100 Poems of 100 Poets). In the Edo period, a matching game using the poems called *uta-garuta* (poem cards) was developed. It eventually developed into a popular New Year parlor game, still played by many families today. There are two sets of pasteboard cards, 100 *yomi-fuda* (reading cards) containing the whole poem and 100 *tori-fuda* (grabbing cards) bearing only the final 14 syllables of the poem. As each poem is read aloud, the contestants have to grab the correct *tori-fuda* from those laid out on the floor. The surprisingly dynamic game is especially popular with women. There is an official association and *Kyogi-karuta*

(Competitive Karuta) contests are shown every January on TV. Since 2007, the interest in competitive karuta has been greatly increased by the popular anime and live-action TV versions of the manga created by Yuki Suetsugu about school karuta teams.

Hanafuda
花札

A card game often played at the New Year is *hanafuda*, also known as *hana-karuta* (flower cards). It developed from Dutch card games introduced in the 16th century and ancient Japanese flower picture matching games. The deck consists of 48 different cards divided into 12 suits, each representing a different month. They are illustrated with bold, stylized pictures—mostly in red, blue and black—of flowers, birds and animals appropriate to each season. The cards are smaller and thicker than playing cards. There are many different rules associated with collecting suits.

Ukiyo-e
浮世絵

The *Ukiyo-e* (pictures of the floating world) genre of art included both paintings and woodblock prints, which are now highly prized by art collectors worldwide. Portraying famous actors, sumo wrestlers, courtesans, legends, and scenes from daily life and famous places, the prints were the equivalent of today's picture postcards, posters and pin-ups, as well as book illustrations. There were also many erotic prints (*shunga*), both for entertainment and instruction. The golden age of Ukiyo-e print production lasted from the 17th century to the late 19th century. The most famous artists are Hiroshige (*53 Stages of the Tokaido*), Hokusai (*36 Views of Mt. Fuji*), Sharaku (Kabuki actors), and Utamaro (beauties).

There are still craftsmen—Japanese and foreign—producing prints in the traditional way, many of them working alone. However, the production of a woodblock print is a long and difficult process, and it used to be a team effort by specialists: the artist (*ukiyo-e-shi*) who produced the original India ink design; the carvers (*hori-shi*) who carved the blocks, usually of cherry wood; the printers (*suri-shi*) who carefully printed each color, ensuring the paper remained perfectly aligned; and the publisher who dealt with distribution.

Noh
能

Masks are a very important part of Noh, the ancient performing art that includes music, chanting, stylistic dancing and actors portraying historical figures, priests, demons and ghosts. The main performer, the *shite*, often wears a wooden mask while performing. Each mask is slightly different and Noh actors can express a huge variety of emotions through their subtle head movements. Amongst the most common types of Noh masks are *ko-omote*, a young woman's mask, and *hannya*, representing a female demon with horns. The eye-holes in the masks are very small, so the actors must move around the stage very carefully, using the wooden pillars as positioning guides.

Kyogen
狂言

Masks also feature in around 50 of the classical repertoire of 260 short Kyogen comic plays that were historically performed between the very serious Noh dramas, but are often presented independently today. Masks are used for animals, including foxes and *tanuki*, and supernatural beings such as gods and devils. The sons of famous

Kyogen actors generally make their demanding stage debut at a very young age dressed in a monkey costume and wearing a mask.

Bunraku
文楽

Dating back 400 years, Bunraku theater is a unique combination of *joruri*—stories narrated and chanted with shamisen accompaniment—and puppets who act out the stories in silence. The main characters are operated by three puppeteers using skilful coordination that takes many years to perfect. Some of the carved wooden heads (*kashira*), operated by the chief puppeteer (*omozukai*), have movable mouths, eyes and eyebrows. There are around 70 types of kashira, including minor characters with faces resembling traditional Japanese masks.

Men
面

Masks (*men*) feature a great deal in Japanese culture—in stage plays, festivals, rituals, folk dances and children's role playing. They are made of wood, metal, papier-mâché and plastic. Humorous masks used in *kagura* Shinto dances include *otafuku*, the fat-cheeked goddess of mirth, and *hyottoko*, a silly man's face with pouting lips. There are also masks of various species of demons, such as *tengu* (long-nosed goblins) and the *oni* (ogres) who appear in the *Setsubun* bean-throwing festival on February 3rd, and the face makeup of Kabuki actors. Masks of manga and anime characters are very popular with children.

Niwa
庭

The long tradition of small, self-contained Japanese gardens (*niwa*) suggesting a whole landscape is alive and well today as a way of making the best use of limited space. They are more for admiring than playing in. Some elements of the gardens around tea ceremony teahouses may be included, such as *tobi-ishi* stepping-stones across gravel or sand, a *sodegaki* ornamental fence adjoining the house, and an *ishidoro* stone lantern. The dry sand, gravel and rock gardens seen at temples are called *karesansui*.

Bonsai
盆栽

The painstaking ancient art of *bonsai* (tray-planting) involves the cultivation of miniature potted trees based on the spirit of *shin-zen-bi* (truth, goodness, beauty). It's an interesting combination of manipulating nature while encouraging an appreciation of nature itself. Bonsai can be seen outside people's houses, in *tokonoma* alcoves

and at exhibitions. The idea is to create dwarf versions of trees—particularly *matsu* (pine), *keyaki* (zelkova), *sugi* (cedar), *momiji* (maple), *sakura* (cherry) and *hinoki* (cypress)—while maintaining proper proportions with the container, a pleasing asymmetry, and a totally 'natural' look. Bonsai can live for hundreds of years, and their image of immortality makes them popular with the elderly.

Kakejiku
掛け軸

A *kakejiku* hanging picture scroll may include a vertical ink-brush landscape painting (*sansui-ga*), a picture of seasonal birds or flowers (*kacho-ga*), Buddhist images (*butsu-ga*), or a fine piece of calligraphy. Only one kakejiku is displayed in the *tokonoma* alcove of a traditional Japanese room (*washitsu*) at any one time, usually chosen for its seasonal relevance. The picture in the center is called the *honshi*, and the decorative mounting is the *hyogu*. The scrolls are rolled up and stored in special boxes when not on display.

Ikebana
生け花

An *ikebana* (flowers kept alive) arrangement of flowers, grasses, leaves and berries, carefully chosen to reflect the season, is placed on the matted floor (*toko*) of a tokonoma alcove. In some cases a simple arrangement may be created in a hanging bamboo vase. An incense burner, a valuable ornament, such as a precious stone or carving, or a bonsai may also be on display. When you enter a washitsu with a tokonoma, it is polite to admire the kakejiku and ikebana display before sitting down.

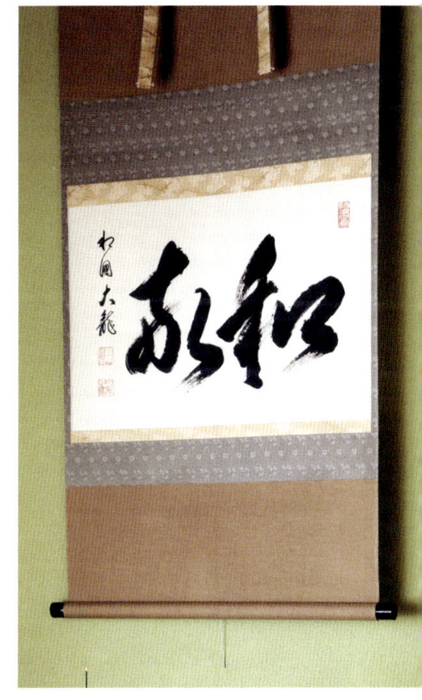

Shiro

城

Japan's distinctive castles (*shiro*) were developed to deal with the military situation around the end of the 16th and early 17th centuries. Their names consist of the location plus the suffix *-jo*. The main difference from European castles is that only the base ramparts were built of stone. The buildings were all wooden, covered with thick clay and plaster as a defense against fire and

attack. However, only a few original structures have survived fires, earthquakes and war damage, so many famous castles, such as Osaka-jo and Nagoya-jo, are actually 20th century reconstructions. The most popular of the dozen or so complete original castle structures that remain today is the beautiful Himeji-jo in Hyogo Prefecture (The White Heron Castle), completed in 1610. It was designated as a World Heritage Site in 1993.

Tenshukaku
天守閣

The high *tenshukaku* keep, or donjon, served as both a watchtower and the last refuge for the lord and his family when a castle was under siege. It was provided with a water supply from a well (*ido*). The two bronze *shachihoko*, mythical creatures like dolphins with lifted tails on the roof of some donjons were believed to protect the castle against fire.

In most cases, an extensive castle town (*jokamachi*) was built around the castle, including temples, entertainment districts and the residences of lower officials. Direct access to the castle was difficult, as castles had at least one wide moat with steep sides (*hori*). In Tokyo, stretches of the inner moat (*uchibori*) and the outer moat (*sotobori*) of Edo Castle can still be seen today, although only a few of the castle's gates (*mon*) remain. The main gate (*ote-mon*) of castles often consisted of two gates at right angles with a square courtyard between them (*masugata*), in which attackers could be ambushed.

 **SPRING**

Momo-no-sekku
桃の節句

The *Momo-no-sekku* (Peach Blossom Festival) celebrated on March 3rd centers around girls. It's also called *Joshi-no-sekku* (Festival of the Day of the Snake in early March) or *Hina-matsuri* (The Doll Festival).

The tradition is to set up a display of ceremonial dolls (*hina-ningyo*) wearing court costumes from the Heian period (794–1192). The idea is to pray for the happiness and health of daughters, as well as encourage good behavior and respect for family and ancestors. Dressed up in their finest kimono, girls admire the display dolls, but don't play with them.

Hina-ningyo
ひな人形

The Hina-ningyo dolls are displayed on a special stand (*hina-dan*), with five or more tiers covered in red cloth or felt. The basic set consists of 15 dolls, depicting an ancient Imperial peach-blossom-viewing party. The top tier features the *o-dairi-sama*, representing the Emperor and Empress in ancient brocade court costumes sitting in front of a gold folded screen. On each side is a *bonbori* floor lamp. On the next tier are three ladies-in-waiting ready to serve sake (*sannin-kanjo*). Below them are five musicians (*gonin-bayashi*), two ministers (*daijin*) with bows and arrows, and finally three footmen (*jicho*), who are sometimes shown as crying, laughing and angry drunks!

Hanami
花見

Since ancient times, the word *hana* (flower) has been synonymous with *sakura* (cherry blossom), which has become the iconic flower of Japan. It's a potent motif for the arrival of spring, blooming around early April in central Japan when so many things start, including the school year. It's also regarded as a symbol of worldly transience, blooming briefly and falling quickly. *Hanami* (cherry-blossom viewing) took off as an entertainment with ordinary townspeople around 400 years ago. They started gathering under the cherry trees to eat, drink and be merry. Since the 19th century, the *Somei-yoshino* flowering cherry has been planted nationwide. Being a clone, all the trees bloom at the same time in each location. As the "cherry front" gradually moves from south to north, plastic sheets and cardboard are spread on the ground and hanami party-time begins!

Koinobori
こいのぼり

May 5th is today a national holiday called Children's Day. But the traditional names for it are *Tango-no-sekku* (Boys' Festival) or *Shobu-no-sekku* (Iris Festival).

Many insects appear in May and farmers used to erect flowing banners in the fields to drive them off the crops. Big banners bearing family crests were erected at their houses by the samurai class to celebrate the birth of sons. Around the end of the 18th century, not to be outdone, the farmers and merchants decided to create their own displays. They developed paper streamers representing carp swimming upstream against the current—tough, fearless and persistent, but calm when about to die. This was the origin of the *koinobori* carp streamers resembling windsocks that are still flown from tall poles by families from around the end of April, usually made of cloth or synthetic material. Since the end of World War Two, the top black carp is said to represent the father, the next shorter red one the mother, and then blue and green ones for sons. Daughters may also be represented these days. Some communities stretch long ropes with many large carp streamers across rivers.

Gogatsu-ningyo
五月人形

Another traditional Boys' Festival custom that continues today is the display of various items related to male strength and bravery (*gogatsu-ningyo*).

In the old days, a boy's fortune could depend greatly on his skill with weapons. In May, the family's heirlooms of armor, helmets, swords, etc, would be brought out for airing, and the father of the family would lecture his sons on the historic deeds of fighting figures of the past. These ranged from actual warriors, such as Hideyoshi and Yoshitsune, to strong legendary boys, such as Momotaro and Kintaro. Pictures and dolls of these characters would also be displayed.

 **SUMMER**

Tanabata-kazari
七夕飾り

The colorful *Tanabata-no-sekku* (Weaving Loom Festival) was formerly held on the 7th day of the 7th month of the lunar calendar. Today it's held on July 7th in most parts of Japan, or one month later. Also called *Hoshi Matsuri* (Star Festival), it originated around the 8th century. It's based on Chinese stories about celestial lovers who were only allowed to cross the Milky Way to meet once a year. The wife was Orihime, a celestial princess who was a skilled weaver (Vega, the Weaver) and her husband was Hikoboshi (Altair, the Cowherd). Tanabata became a popular festival for all ages during the Edo period. Wishes are written on long colored strips of paper (*tanzaku*), which are hung from a bamboo branch.

Hanabi
花火

Japanese fireworks (*hanabi*, flower fire) are now regarded as the finest in the world. *Hanabi* are an integral part of Japanese summer festivities, both in the form of massive displays (*hanabi-taikai*) and small personal parties in gardens and streets. To the Japanese, there is something refreshing and even 'cooling' about fireworks on hot, humid summer evenings. Large displays are held nationwide in July and August, many of them above rivers or the sea, where there is a pleasant breeze and beautiful reflections in the water. They feature a great variety of exquisite *uchiage-hanabi*, giant bursts of color, as well as *shikake-hanabi*, set piece fireworks with special effects.

Mikoshi
神輿

Intricately carved *mikoshi* (deity palanquin) portable shrines play a major role in festivals for taking the local god on a tour of the neighborhood to give a divine blessing. They can weigh up to several tons and need hundreds of men and, increasingly, women to carry them on wooden poles, a joint effort mirroring the traditional communal work in fields. The shaking movements are said to reflect the power of the enshrined deity, not just the enthusiasm and inebriation of the bearers.

The mikoshi are usually made of wood with black lacquer and gilding. They are rather like small shrine buildings, with miniature *torii* gates, steps, and a complex roof topped by a gold phoenix (*hoo*). Other mikoshi are tiny and pulled along on carts by children.

Bon-kazari
盆飾り

The three-day *O-Bon* (or *Urabon-e*) festival in July or August welcomes back the spirits of the dead for their annual visit. Basically a Buddhist festival, but also connected with Shinto ancestor worship, it's a mixture of fond memories and ancestor respect with lively communal events such as *Bon-odori* dances. *Bon-chochin* lanterns are set up in the house and small offerings of

the spirits' favorite food are made on a *shoryo-dana* (spirit altar). On the final day, simple vegetable dolls with toothpicks or chosticks for legs are placed outside the house: a cucumber horse for the spirit to ride on, and an egg plant ox to carry all the baggage.

Sensu
扇子

Fans have long been connected with the decorative and performing arts as well as daily life. It's said that the first Chinese fans in Japan did not fold. The Japanese claim to have invented *sensu* folding fans more than a thousand

years ago, based on a study of the wings of bats. Since then they have acquired many different functions as well as being a canvas for all kinds of paintings and calligraphy and an intrinsic part of theater performances, *rakugo* storytelling, *buyo* Japanese dance, and the tea ceremony. The basic structure of a *sensu* is up to 25 bamboo ribs covered with folded *washi* paper. Some are made entirely of scented wood or use silk instead of paper.

Uchiwa
うちわ

Flat, often circular, fans are called *uchiwa*. They have long been used for advertising purposes, and plastic-ribbed versions are commonly handed out at station exits in summer. Uchiwa come in very handy to stick down the back of a *yukata* (summer kimono) belt. They can also be used like bellows for barbecues and for cooling ingredients such as sushi rice or boiled vegetables. Sumo referees hold a wooden version of the iron *gunbai-uchiwa* once used for giving commands by war commanders.

Sudare & Yoshizu
すだれ／よしず

In the days before air-conditioning and electric fans, the Japanese devised various types of blinds and screens to keep their houses cool in the fierce heat of the sun, provide some kind of breeze, and cut out direct sunlight. The general name for bamboo blinds is *sudare* and reed screens are called *yoshizu*. The ideal materials are not affected by humidity and are preferably grown in Japan, because they tend to be more resistant to mold than imported materials.

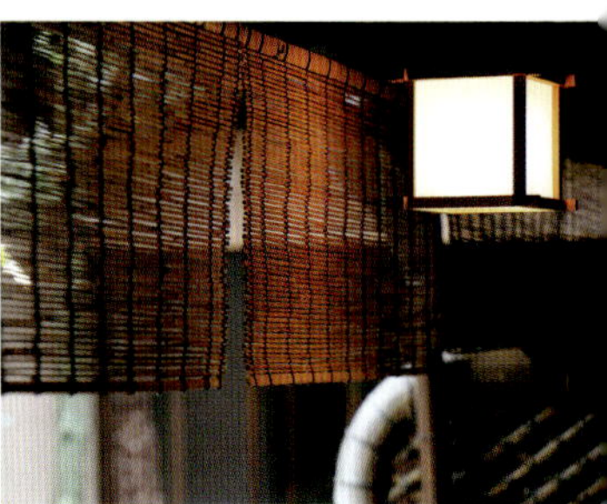

Kakigori
かき氷

Ice was once a rare commodity, only available to the aristocracy who could pay for its transport from northern mountain areas. Japanese travelers overseas in the late 19th century discovered ice cream. It soon became possible to produce ice and one of today's favorite Japanese summer treats—*kakigori* (shaved ice).

Wherever you go in summer, you will see small red, white and blue flags bearing the character for 'ice.' This usually means that ice-cream and kakigori are on sale. You will find it at convenience stores (sometimes ready packed), on beaches, and at festivals, and many people make their own at home.

Kaya
蚊帳

At one time mosquito nets (*kaya*) were an essential part of daily life. Square in shape, they were hung by four corners from the ceiling and fixed to pegs on the floor, filling most of the room. There were smaller versions with a bamboo frame for young children. Kaya have gradually become unnecessary thanks to improved construction methods, better fitting windows and doors, the introduction of air-conditioning, and the sliding metal-framed *amido* (mosquito-netting doors) that run on rails outside windows. However, kaya made of hemp or polyester that hang loose to the floor can still be bought for use in old houses or for camping.

Katori-senko
蚊取り線香

If you want to keep the doors and windows open in summer or sit outside, then it's advisable to use some sort of mosquito repellent. The traditional style called *katori-senko* consists of slow-burning coils of hard green incense made from pyrethrum chrysanthemum petals. They usually come in a tin with a short metal stand to hold the coil in the air as it burns, and last for about 10 hours. Earthenware containers shaped like a fat pig have long been popular for holding the coils. There are modern electric versions for use in closed rooms that exude insect-killing fumes from small mats or liquid, and various miniature portable mosquito-repellent devices, including wristbands and ultrasonic keyholders.

Furin
風鈴

There are many traditional ways to help the mind and body forget the heat and humidity of mid-summer in Japan, including lots of chilling ghost stories on TV and the Kabuki stage. Another charming and inexpensive way is to hang a small *furin* wind-bell from the eaves of the house or an adjacent tree. The tinkling noise, created by a puff of breeze, somehow helps you feel a little cooler. Dating back to the 14th century, furin can be made of glass, porcelain, bamboo or metal. Attached to the clapper is something to catch the wind—usually a long piece of paper, or even a feather.

 **AUTUMN**

Momiji-gari
紅葉狩り

Much of Japan is mountainous and forested, and there are large numbers of deciduous broadleaved trees that change color in autumn, especially *momiji* (maples) which turn red and *icho* (gingkoes) which turn yellow. The Japanese have long loved the beauty of the autumn colors (*koyo*). In the Heian period in the 11th century, aristocrats would gather to view them and write appreciative but wistful poems. This was known as *momiji-gari* (maple hunting) and it spread to the common people from around the 16th century. The roads leading to famous momiji-gari locations, such as Nikko in Tochigi Prefecture, feature major traffic jams in October and November as everyone hunts for the best views.

Tsukimi
月見

In Japan, a full moon has no connection with lunacy or werewolves, but only with peace and beauty. In the past, *tsukimi* (moon-viewing) parties were held on *Jugoya* (15th Night of the 8th Month) and *Jusanya* (13th Night of the 9th Month) according to the old lunar calendar. Guests would write moon-related poems while eating and drinking. Tsukimi are still held on the evenings of a full harvest moon (*chushu no meigetsu*) in September and October.

A *sanpo* offering tray is placed on a table facing the direction the moon will appear with items offered to the Moon Goddess. They include a vase of *susuki* (pampas grass) stalks, two flasks of sake, *tsukimi-dango* (rice-flour dumplings), and two candles. There will also be assorted seasonal fruits and vegetables, such as *kaki* (persimmons), *edamame* (boiled soybeans), *kuri* (chestnuts) and *satoimo* (taro).

Shichi-go-san
七五三

The charming and colorful family festival called *Shichi-go-san* (7-5-3) is held at major shrines nationwide in November. Girls (and sometimes boys) aged three, boys aged five, and girls aged seven are dressed up in their finest clothes (*haregi*) and taken to the shrine to pray for good health and a long life. There is a short purification ceremony and a priest reads out the children's names to the deity to give thanks and ask for protection. It's derived from ancient customs in samurai and merchant families to help children survive childhood: from three they could grow their hair, and girls had it tied up (*kamioki*); boys would wear a *hakama* (pleated skirt) from five (*hakamagi*); and girls would wear a proper *obi* (sash) when they were seven (*obitoki* or *himo-otoshi*).

Chitose-ame
千歳飴

After the 7-5-3 ceremony, the children are given long paper bags (*kesho-bukuro*) contained long red and white sticks of *chitose-ame* (1,000-year candy) made from boiled *mizu-ame* (thick malt syrup). The bags are colorfully decorated with many old symbols of long life and good fortune: pine trees, bamboo and plum blossom (together known as *sho-chiku-bai*), cranes, turtles, *noshi*, the sun's rays, Daikoku's lucky hammer, *daruma*, coral, dice, and maybe a picture of Kintaro, the strong boy from old folk tales.

Botamochi & Ohagi
ぼたもち（おはぎ）

Special rice cakes are prepared for both the spring equinox (*Haru-no-higan*) and the autumn equinox (*Aki-no-higan*). They have different names because of their resemblance to seasonal flowers: *botamochi* (*botan*=peony) in spring and *ohagi* (*hagi*=bush clover) in autumn. They're made from a mixture of steamed rice and *mochigome* (glutinous rice). The ground rice is formed into egg-shaped rice cakes that are covered with red *an* (*azuki* bean paste). A coating of *kinako* (soybean flour) or *kuro-goma* (black sesame) is often added.

Kadomatsu
門松

Christmas decorations disappear in Japan as soon as December 25th comes round because there are so many traditional New Year decorations. An important one placed outside private houses and shops is the *kadomatsu* (gate pine). It represents a landmark to welcome the god of the next year (*toshigami*). Pine branches are used because they are strong and evergreen, suggesting longevity. Ideally, there should be a kadomatsu display on both sides of the entrance: one with a smooth branch of pine (=female); and one with a rough branch with the bark left on (=male).

In its simplest form, the kadomatsu is just a pine branch fixed to the side of the front door. But a full display consists of several important elements that symbolize a long and prosperous life. For example, stalks of bamboo, diagonally sliced at the top like spears symbolize virtue, constancy, and rapid, healthy growth. *Habotan* (ornamental kale) is often included to add some color.

Shime-kazari
しめ飾り

Shime-kazari is the term for the New Year decorations full of symbolism that are hung in various places, such as over the entrance to a house. The shime-kazari indicate to the god of the New Year (*toshigami*) that a temporary abode has been created and purified. The base of the decoration is a version of the *shimenawa* twisted sacred ropes seen at Shinto shrines, which symbolize purity. Other common elements are also used in *kagami-mochi* displays inside the house, such as fern fronds (*urajiro*) and dried kelp (*konbu*).

Mochitsuki
もちつき

Shortly before the end of the year, many people enjoy pounding hot boiled glutinous rice for making *mochi* rice cakes, an essential element of New Year cuisine. This tradition is called *mochitsuki*.

The old way—claimed to produce the most delicious mochi—is to use a large mortar (*usu*) and a heavy, long-handled wooden mallet (*kine*). The mortars are around one meter high and made of a solid piece of wood or stone hollowed out in the center. Unlike the smaller *suribachi* kitchen mortars, they're smooth inside. The mallet is slammed down on to the dough with an over-the-shoulder action, like chopping wood with an axe. This is done rhythmically, with another person adding water by hand and turning the dough between each blow. It's an exhausting and dangerous operation: a mistimed blow can smash the helper's hand. At some public events, such as the Harvest Festival on November 23rd, you can watch professionals performing the dangerous high-speed 'team mochitsuki'!

Kagami-mochi
鏡もち

Mochi rice balls are a major celebratory feature of New Year cuisine because the sound of 'mochi' suggests another word meaning 'long-lasting.' They're not only displayed but also eaten in various ways. When it became normal to construct *tokonoma* alcoves in houses in the Muromachi Period (1336–1573), the custom began of displaying mochi in them as an *osonae* (offering to the unseen) and a prayer for good fortune.

Today, two round *kagami-mochi* (mirror rice-cakes) with flat bottoms are placed on top of each other on a plain wooden *sanpo* stand. The display usually includes some *konbu* (kelp), a *daidai* (bitter orange) or a *mikan* (mandarin), *urajiro* (fern leaves), and a skewer of dried *kaki* (persimmons). A ceremony called *kagami-biraki* (opening the mirror) is held on January 11th to break up the hardened rice balls and eat them.

Toshikoshi-soba
年越しそば

December 31st, which launches the start of the important New Year celebrations, is called *omisoka*. It's a custom for families to eat hot buckwheat noodles (*toshikoshi-soba*) in the evening before midnight (but not after). The name literally means 'year-crossing noodles'—in other words, seeing out the old year and welcoming in the new. Various reasons are given for this custom. One common explanation is that the length of

soba noodles symbolizes longevity. Another is that soba is easy to cut, so it symbolizes the cutting off of all the hardships, troubles and debts of the year just ending.

Joya-no-kane
除夜の鐘

Japanese temple bells are rung 108 times (*joya-no-kane*) on New Year's Eve or early on January 1st. This represents driving away the 108 sins of the world and starting the new year fresh and pure. In the old days, the 108th ring would coincide with midnight. However, in recent years a Western-style 'countdown' to midnight has even spread to some major temples, and the first ring marks midnight. At many temples, it's possible to apply in advance to be one of the bell-ringers for a small contribution.

Hatsu-mode
初詣

The first visit of the year to a temple or shrine is called *hatsu-mode*. Some people like to combine it with the countdown to midnight on December 31st. Others prefer to see the New Year in at home and then head out, or go during one of the first three days of January, which are called *san-ga-nichi*. Only January 1st is a national holiday, but many people take at least three days' holiday. In the case of major shrines such as Tsurugaoka Hachimangu in Kamakura and Meiji Jingu in Tokyo, several million people visit during this period every year. Progress toward the main buildings is extremely slow! Huge *saisenbako* money boxes are prepared so that visitors can throw money and then pray for a successful year.

Hamaya
破魔矢

One of the most popular lucky charms on sale at shrines at the New Year are wooden arrows called *hamaya*. Said to be swift and sure carriers of good fortune that help to preserve a house or business against evil and all kinds of calamity during the coming year, they are usually kept in a high position above a doorway or window. Generally

around 60 centimeters long, they have white synthetic feathers, but not a sharp tip. Red, white, gold or silver paper is wrapped around the shaft, bearing the shrine's name. There may also be small bells and an *ema* votive tablet attached. The idea is to buy a new *hamaya* every year and take the one from the previous year for burning at the shrine it came from.

O-toso
おとそ

For more than 1,000 years, a special type of sweet sake called *o-toso* (defeat evil) has been drunk on the morning of January 1st and offered to guests over the holiday period. It's regarded as a protection against sickness and evil. The recipe varies around Japan, but basically consists of sake or *mirin* (sweet cooking sake), spiced with medicinal herbs, including Japanese pepper (*sansho*), ginger, rhubarb, cinnamon and cassia bark. A suitable mixture of herbs used to be given out as a New Year gift from doctors and pharmacies. Today most people buy a ready-prepared teabag of spices to add to some sake on New Year's Eve and leave overnight. It's served into lacquered sake cups (*sakazuki*) from a decorative flask, such as a *kyusu* teapot.

O-toshidama
お年玉

Gifts of money called *o-toshidama* (year jewels) are a main attraction of the New Year for children. Until the 20th century, Japan had no general tradition of giving individuals birthday or Christmas presents. This custom developed from several ancient practices: families

exchanging presents at the New Year; shrines and temples distributing gifts they had themselves received; and the custom of the oldest member of a family representing the god of the New Year (*toshigami*) by presenting to the younger members of the family the *mochi* rice cakes that had been dedicated to the god. Today, relatives and family friends present children with special decorated envelopes (*o-toshidama-bukuro*) containing money.

O-sechi-ryori
おせち料理

Various special food items are served at the New Year, both for the family and guests. One of them is *zoni*, a hot soup containing *mochi*, pieces of chicken, citron peel, etc. Usually a clear soup in the Kanto and Kyushu regions, it's often made with *miso* (fermented soybean paste) in Kansai. The traditional mixture of symbolic seafood, meat, vegetable and pickled dishes is called *o-sechi-ryori*. The items can all be made in advance and eaten cold, giving housewives and househusbands a welcome rest from kitchen work. Only the soup and the rice need

to be served hot. However, it's now common to order *o-sechi-ryori* from restaurants or shops, often including non-traditional items such as Chinese dishes or sushi. And some people prefer not to eat the same items for three days!

Kamakura
かまくら

In the snowy areas of northern Japan there's a tradition for children to build round *kamakura* snow houses like small igloos. There's room inside for three or four children to sit on cushions on thin straw mats (*mushiro*). Lighting is traditionally provided by candles, but today many are fitted with electric lighting and even a *kotatsu* heated table. However, children still often sit around a small *hibachi* charcoal heater and grill *mochi* rice cakes. A small recess is made in the back wall for a miniature *kamidana* shrine dedicated to Suijin, the God of Water, and prayers are offered for ample spring rain. If the door is covered with a *sudare* screen, it can be quite warm inside and some children even stay in the kamakura overnight.

Stuart Varnam-Atkin

Born in Birmingham in the U.K. and a graduate of Oxford University, he has lived in Japan since the 1970s as a writer, actor, TV presenter and narrator. In 1991, he co-founded Birmingham Brains Trust (BBT), a narration and translation agency. He was a co-presenter of the *Trad Japan* series and the narrator on *Begin Japanology* (NHK Educational TV) and has written and presented TV courses for the Open University of Japan. From 2018 to 2021, he presented *Discover Bunraku* from the stage of the National Theatre in Tokyo, and for many years he has been the narrator of *Japan Video Topics* (the Ministry of Foreign Affairs). His publications include *Who Invented Natto?*, *Are Japanese Cats Left-Handed?*, *Stories from The Tale of Genji*, *15 Tales from Shakespeare* (IBC), *Trad Japan Mod Nippon* (NHK), and co-translations of Miyazawa Kenji stories (IBC) and several Japanese manga, including *The Tale of Genji* and *Chihayafuru* (Kodansha).

The Best of Japanese Culture

2024年9月6日　第1刷発行

著　　者　　ステュウット ヴァーナム−アットキン

発 行 者　　賀川　洋

発 行 所　　IBCパブリッシング株式会社
　　　　　　〒162-0804
　　　　　　東京都新宿区中里町29番3号
　　　　　　菱秀神楽坂ビル
　　　　　　TEL 03-3513-4511
　　　　　　FAX 03-3513-4512
　　　　　　www.ibcpub.co.jp

印 刷 所　　株式会社シナノパブリッシングプレス

ISBN 978-4-7946-0836-9

Printed in Japan

Photographs:
Stuart Varnam-Atkin (p.18, p.21, p.25 (both), p.26, p.39 (lower), p.41)
Mitsuo Tsukada (p.6, p.10, p.11 (lower), p.15, p.16 (upper), p.19, p.23 (upper), p.31, p.47, p.56, p.61, p.74, Back cover)
Adobe Stock, photolibrary, PIXTA, MIXA, 素材辞典, Wikipedia, IBC編集部